Plows

Lori Dittmer

CREATIVE EDUCATION
CREATIVE PAPERBACKS

seedlings

Published by Creative Education and Creative Paperbacks
P.O. Box 227, Mankato, Minnesota 56002
Creative Education and Creative Paperbacks
are imprints of The Creative Company
www.thecreativecompany.us

Design by Ellen Huber; production by Joe Kahnke
Art direction by Rita Marshall
Printed in the United States of America

Photographs by Alamy (Alan Keith Beastall, Realimage, Stephen
Sykes), iStockphoto (valio84sl), Minden Pictures (Richard Becker),
Shutterstock (ae ssp, arogant, B Brown, risteski goce, Anatoliy
Kosolapov, J. Lekavicius, Lurin, somsak nitimongkolchai,
Orientaly, Catalin Petolea, Perutskyi Petro, Deyana Stefanova
Robova, safakcakir), SuperStock (Juice Images)

Library of Congress Cataloging-in-Publication Data
Names: Dittmer, Lori, author.
Title: Plows / Lori Dittmer.
Series: Seedlings.
Includes bibliographical references and index.
Summary: A kindergarten-level introduction to plows,
covering their purpose, parts, role in farming, and such
defining features as their heavy blades.
Identifiers: ISBN 978-1-60818-910-6 (hardcover) / ISBN 978-1-
62832-526-3 (pbk) / ISBN 978-1-56660-962-3 (eBook)
This title has been submitted for CIP
processing under LCCN 2017940114.

CCSS: RI.K.1, 2, 3, 4, 5, 6, 7;
RI.1.1, 2, 3, 4, 5, 6, 7; RF.K.1, 3; RF.1.1

First Edition HC 9 8 7 6 5 4 3 2 1
First Edition PBK 9 8 7 6 5 4 3 2 1

TABLE OF CONTENTS

Hello, plows!

Plows are farm machines. They hook on to tractors. Tractors pull them through fields.

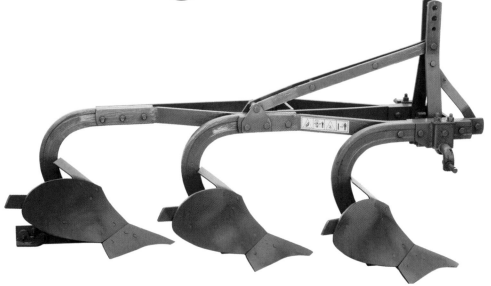

Plows dig furrows. They turn dirt over. This buries weeds and old crops.

Now farmers can plant new crops.

Heavy metal blades slice through soil.

Some blades go just a few inches deep. Others dig down more than a foot (0.3 m).

Some plows do different jobs. Chisel plows rip deep into the ground.

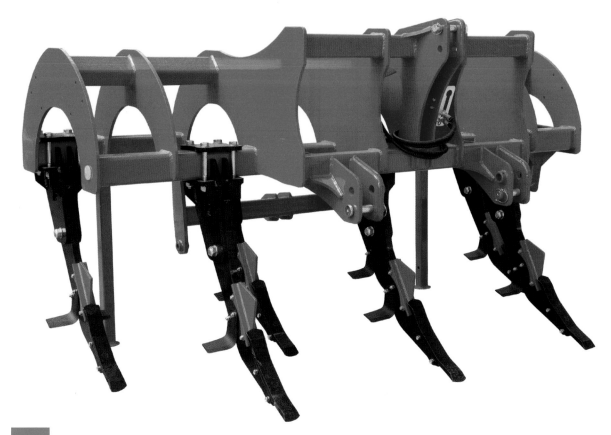

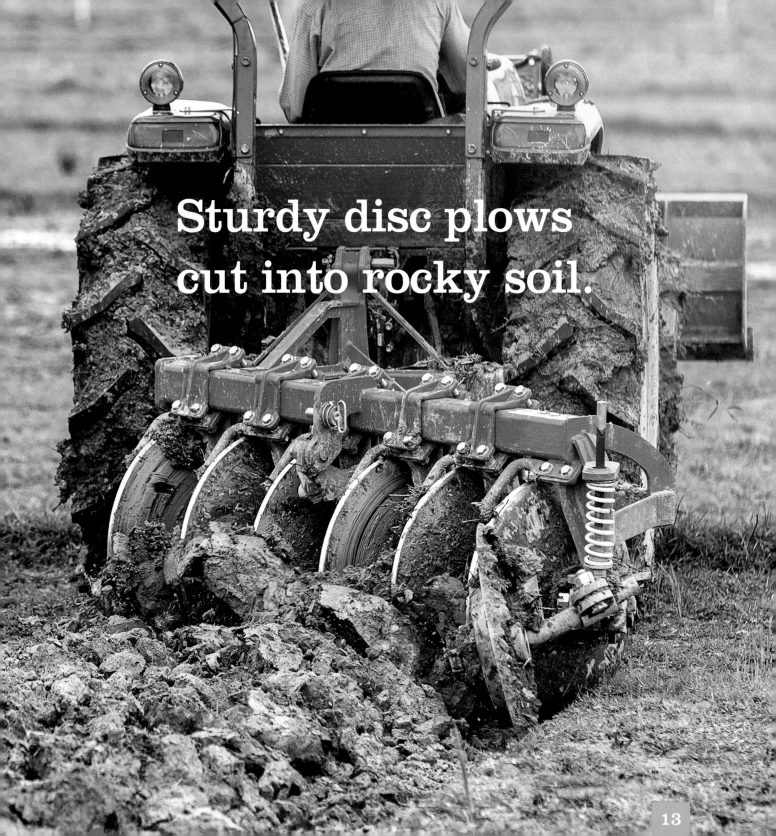

Sturdy disc plows cut into rocky soil.

Too much plowing can lead to erosion. Some farmers limit how much they plow.

Plows break up hard dirt. They make new fields. They get land ready to plant.

Goodbye, plows!

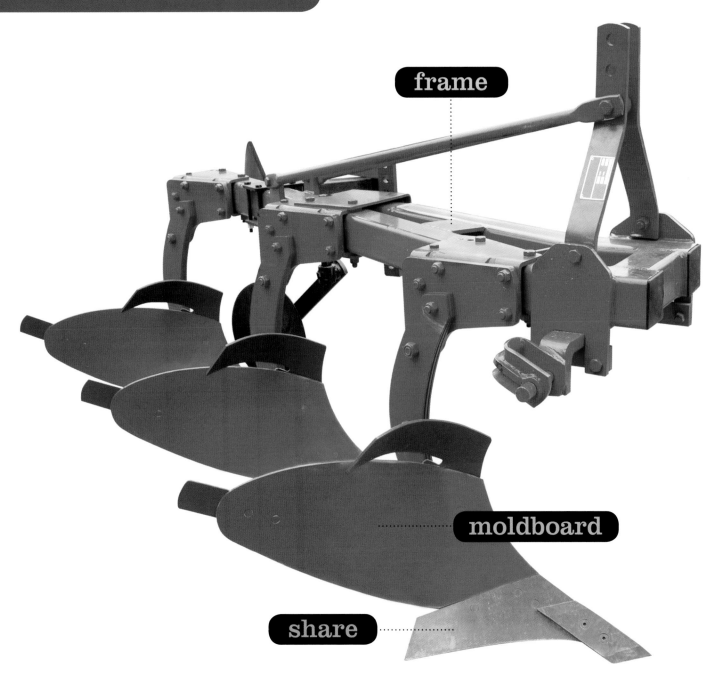

frame

moldboard

share

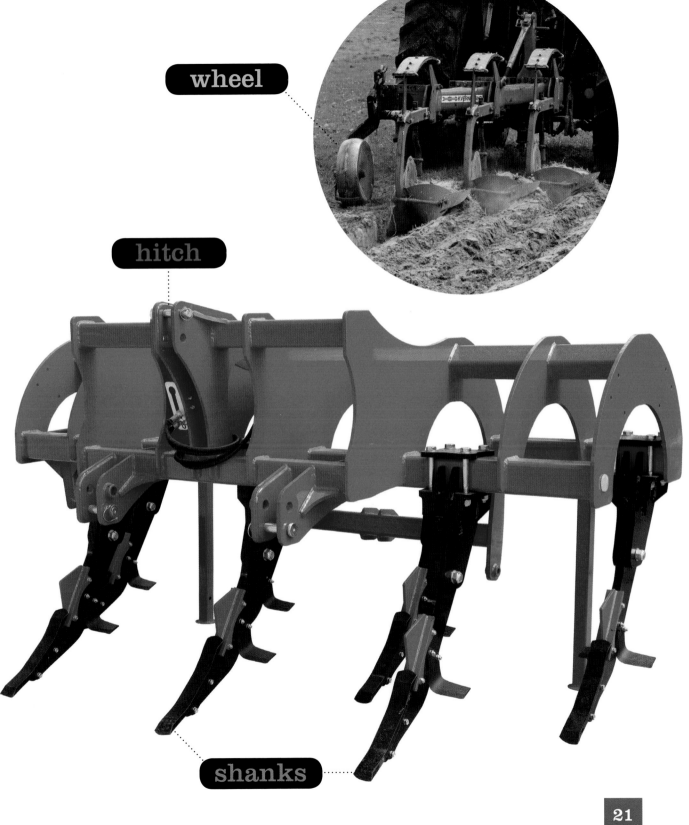

wheel

hitch

shanks

Words to Know

crops: plants that are grown for people or animals to eat and use

erosion: where land is worn away by forces such as water and wind

furrows: straight, narrow rows for planting seeds

soil: the layer of earth in which plants grow

Read More

Dieker, Wendy. *Tractors.*
Minneapolis: Jump!, 2013.

West, David. *Farm Machinery.*
Mankato, Minn.: Smart Apple Media, 2015.

Websites

Kids Farm
http://www.kidsfarm.com/wheredo.htm
Learn about farm equipment and animals from a farm
in Colorado.

Tractors for Kids – Learn Farm Vehicles
and Equipment with Blippi
https://www.youtube.com/watch?v=ZyEnVLPhjUc
Watch a video to learn more about farm machines.

Index